First World War
and Army of Occupation
War Diary
France, Belgium and Germany

29 DIVISION
Divisional Troops
Divisional Ammunition Column
1 March 1916 - 31 October 1919

WO95/2292/4

The Naval & Military Press Ltd
www.nmarchive.com
Published in association with The National Archives

Published by

The Naval & Military Press Ltd

Unit 10 Ridgewood Industrial Park,

Uckfield, East Sussex,

TN22 5QE England

Tel: +44 (0) 1825 749494

www.naval-military-press.com

www.nmarchive.com

This diary has been reprinted in facsimile from the original. Any imperfections are inevitably reproduced and the quality may fall short of modern type and cartographic standards.

© Crown Copyright
Images reproduced by permission of The National Archives, London, England, 2015.

Contents

Document type	Place/Title	Date From	Date To
Heading	WO95/2292/4 Divisional Ammunition Column		
Heading	29th Division Divl Artillery 29th Divl Ammn Column Mar 1916-Oct 1919		
Heading	Originally 53rd (Welch) Divisional A.C. 29th Divisional Ammunition Column March 1916 Dec 18		
Heading	War Diary of 29th Division Ammn Col. 53rd (Welsh) Divl Ammn Col From March 1st 1916 To March 31st 1916 Volume 3/1916		
War Diary	Rebecq	01/03/1916	24/03/1916
War Diary	Bergeneuse	24/03/1916	25/03/1916
War Diary	Bonnieres	25/03/1916	26/03/1916
War Diary	Talmas	26/03/1916	28/03/1916
War Diary	Caumesnil	28/03/1916	31/03/1916
War Diary	Arqueves	31/03/1916	31/03/1916
Heading	29th Divisional Ammunition Column April 1916		
Heading	War Diary of 29th Divisional Ammn. Col. Base 53 (Welsh) Divl A.C. From April 1st 1916 To April 30th 1916 Volume 4/1916		
War Diary	Arqueves	01/04/1916	17/04/1916
Heading	29th Divisional Ammunition Column May 1916		
Heading	War Diary From 1/5/16 To 31/5/16 29 Div Amm Col Vol 5		
War Diary	Arqueves	01/05/1916	26/05/1916
War Diary	Amplier	31/05/1916	31/05/1916
Heading	29th Divisional Ammunition Column June 1916		
War Diary	Amplier	01/06/1916	17/06/1916
War Diary	Acheux	20/06/1916	30/06/1916
Heading	29th Divisional Ammunition Column July 1916		
War Diary	Acheux	01/07/1916	01/07/1916
War Diary	Amplier	06/07/1916	31/07/1916
Heading	29th Divisional Ammunition Column August 1916		
War Diary	Amplier	01/08/1916	09/08/1916
War Diary	Acheux	10/08/1916	31/08/1916
Heading	29th Divisional Ammunition Column September 1916		
Heading	War Diary of 29th Divisional Ammn. Column From 1-9-16 To 30-9-16 Volume 5		
War Diary	Acheux	01/09/1916	12/09/1916
War Diary	Poperinghe	13/09/1916	30/09/1916
Heading	29th Divisional Ammunition Column October 1916		
Heading	29th Divisional Ammunition Column		
Heading	War Diary of 29th Divisional Ammunition Column From 1st October 1916 To 31st October 1916 (Volume 6)		
War Diary	Poperinghe	01/10/1916	01/10/1916
War Diary	Herzeele	08/10/1916	10/10/1916
War Diary	Daours	11/10/1916	12/10/1916
War Diary	Bazentin-Le Grand	14/10/1916	31/10/1916
Heading	29th Divisional Ammunition Column November 1916		
Heading	War Diary of 29th Divisional Ammunition Column From 1st Nov 1916 To 30th Nov 1916 (Volume No 7)		

War Diary	Bazentin Le-Grand	01/11/1916	01/11/1916
War Diary	Meaulte	26/11/1916	26/11/1916
War Diary	Carnoy	29/11/1916	30/11/1916
War Diary	Albert	01/11/1916	01/11/1916
War Diary	Corbie	02/11/1916	16/11/1916
War Diary	Carnoy	17/11/1916	29/11/1916
Heading	29th Divisional Ammunition Column December 1916		
Heading	War Diary of 29th Divisional Ammunition Column From 1st December 1916 To 31st December 1916 (Volume 8)		
War Diary	Carnoy	01/12/1916	31/12/1916
Heading	War Diary of 29th Divisional Ammunition Column From 1st January 1917 To 31st January 1917 (Volume 9)		
War Diary	Carnoy	01/01/1917	31/01/1917
Heading	War Diary of 29th Divisional Ammunition Column From 1st February 1917 To 28th February 1917 (Volume 10)		
War Diary	Carnoy	01/02/1917	28/02/1917
Heading	War Diary of 29th Divisional Ammunition Column From 1st March 1917 To 31st March 1917 (Volume 11)		
War Diary	Carnoy	01/03/1917	01/03/1917
War Diary	Morlancourt	21/03/1917	21/03/1917
War Diary	La Houssoye	23/03/1917	23/03/1917
War Diary	Havernas	24/03/1917	24/03/1917
War Diary	Beauvoir Riviere	26/03/1917	26/03/1917
War Diary	Grand Bouret	27/03/1917	27/03/1917
War Diary	Gouves	28/03/1917	31/03/1917
Heading	War Diary of 29th Divl Ammunition Column From 1st April 1917 To 31st April 1917 (Volume 11)		
War Diary	Gouves	01/04/1917	08/04/1917
War Diary	Arras	11/04/1917	30/04/1917
Heading	War Diary of 29th Divisional Ammunition Column From 1-5-17 To 31-5-17 (Volume No. 18)		
War Diary	Arras	01/05/1917	31/05/1917
Heading	War Diary of 29th Divisional Amm Column From 1-6-17 To 30-6-17 Volume 14		
War Diary	Arras	01/06/1917	30/06/1917
Heading	War Diary of 29th Divisional Ammunition Column From 1-7-17 To 31-7-17 (Volume XV)		
War Diary	Gouves	01/07/1917	01/07/1917
War Diary	Etree Wamin	01/07/1917	02/07/1917
War Diary	Croix	03/07/1917	04/07/1917
War Diary	Nedon & Nedon	04/07/1917	04/07/1917
War Diary	Chelle Neufpre & Environs of Aire	05/07/1917	06/07/1917
War Diary	Staple Godeawaes	07/07/1917	07/07/1917
War Diary	Velde	08/07/1917	31/07/1917
Heading	War Diary of 29th Divl Ammunition Column (Volume No. 18)		
Heading	War Diary of 29th Divl Ammunition Column From 1/8/17 To 31/8/17 (Volume No. 16)		
War Diary	International Corner	01/08/1917	14/08/1917
War Diary	(B.7.d.2.3) Nr Elverdinghe	31/08/1917	31/08/1917
Heading	War Diary of 29th Divisional Amm Column 1-9-17 30-9-17 (Volume No. 17)		
War Diary	(B.7.d.2.3) Near Elverdinghe	01/09/1917	25/09/1917

War Diary	(A 12) Near Elverdinghe	30/09/1917	30/09/1917
War Diary	B.7.d.2.3 Near Elverdinghe	01/10/1917	24/10/1917
War Diary	Doullens	25/10/1917	25/10/1917
War Diary	Amplier	31/10/1917	31/10/1917
Heading	War Diary of 29th Divl Amm Column From 1-11-17 To 30-11-17 (Volume No. 19)		
War Diary	Amplier	01/11/1917	12/11/1917
War Diary	Ville-Sous Ancre	13/11/1917	14/11/1917
War Diary	Camp V C 3	30/11/1917	30/11/1917
Heading	War Diary of 29th Divisional Ammunition Column From 1-12-17 To 31-12-17 Volume No. 20		
War Diary	Camp V.C.3 Nr Equancourt	01/12/1917	14/12/1917
War Diary	Treux	17/12/1917	17/12/1917
War Diary	Acheux	20/12/1917	21/12/1917
War Diary	Gazaincourt	23/12/1917	24/12/1917
War Diary	Offin	31/12/1917	31/12/1917
Heading	War Diary of 29th Divl Amm Column From 1/1/18 To 31/1/18 (Volume No. 21)		
War Diary	Offin	01/01/1918	03/01/1918
War Diary	Verchocq	04/01/1918	04/01/1918
War Diary	Merk St. Lievin	11/01/1918	11/01/1918
War Diary	Renescure	12/01/1918	12/01/1918
War Diary	Oudezeele	13/01/1918	13/01/1918
War Diary	Busse Boom	21/01/1918	21/01/1918
War Diary	Vlamertinghe	31/01/1918	31/01/1918
Heading	War Diary of 29th Divl Amm Column From 1-2-18 To 28-2-18 Volume No. 22		
War Diary	Vlamertinghe	01/02/1918	31/03/1918
Heading	29th Divisional Artillery 29th Divisional Ammunition Column R.F.A. April 1918		
Heading	War Diary of 29th Div Amm Column From 1-4-18 To 30-4-18 Volume No. 24		
War Diary	Vlamertinghe	01/04/1918	25/04/1918
War Diary	Hamhoek	30/04/1918	30/04/1918
Heading	War Diary of 29th Divl Ammunition Column From 1/5/18 To 31/5/18 Volume No. 25		
War Diary	Hamhoek	01/05/1918	31/05/1918
Heading	War Diary 29th Divisional Ammunition Column From June 1st 1918 To June 30th 1918 Volume No. 26		
War Diary	Sercus	01/06/1918	30/06/1918
Heading	War Diary of 29th Divl Amm Column From 1/7/18 To 31/7/18 Volume No. 27		
War Diary	Sercus	01/07/1918	03/07/1918
War Diary	A.3.d.6.9	22/07/1918	22/07/1918
War Diary	Coin Perdu	25/07/1918	31/07/1918
Heading	War Diary of 29th Divisional Ammunition Column From 1/8/18 To 31/8/18 Volume No. 28		
War Diary	Coin Perdu	01/08/1918	31/08/1918
Heading	War Diary of 29th Divisional Ammunition Column 1-9-18 To 30-9-18 Volume 29		
War Diary	Near Hondegham	01/09/1918	30/09/1918
Heading	War Diary of 29th Divisional Amm Column 1/10/18 To 31/10/18 Volume No. 30		
War Diary		01/10/1918	31/10/1918
Heading	War Diary 29th Divl Amm Column Vol November 1918		

War Diary	In The Field	01/11/1918	30/11/1918
Heading	War Diary of 29th Divisional Ammunition Column From 1/12/18 To 31/12/18 Volume No. 32		
War Diary	Comblain Faron	01/12/1918	01/12/1918
War Diary	Aywaille	04/12/1918	04/12/1918
War Diary	Stavelot	05/12/1918	06/12/1918
War Diary	Malmedy	07/12/1918	07/12/1918
War Diary	Kalterherberg	08/12/1918	08/12/1918
War Diary	Simmerath	09/12/1918	09/12/1918
War Diary	Zulpich	10/12/1918	10/12/1918
War Diary	Barren Rath	13/12/1918	13/12/1918
War Diary	Delbrich	21/12/1918	21/12/1918
War Diary	Berg Gladbach	31/12/1918	31/12/1918
Heading	Rhine Army Southern Division Late 29th Division Divisional Ammunition Column Jan-Oct 1919		
Heading	War Diary of 29th Divl Ammn. Col. From 1st To 31st Jany 1918 Volume No. 33 Jan-Oct 19		
War Diary	Berg Gladbach	01/01/1919	31/01/1919
Heading	War Diary of 29th Divisional Ammunition Column February 1919 Volume XXXVII		
War Diary	Berg Gladbach	01/02/1919	22/07/1919
War Diary	Bergisch Gladbach	31/08/1919	31/08/1919
War Diary	Paffrath	31/08/1919	31/08/1919
War Diary	Bergisch Gladbach	19/08/1919	19/08/1919
War Diary	Bergisch Gladbach	18/08/1919	30/09/1919
War Diary	Paffrath	30/09/1919	30/09/1919
War Diary	Bergisch Gladbach	08/09/1919	25/09/1919
War Diary		24/09/1919	24/09/1919
War Diary		18/09/1919	18/09/1919
War Diary		31/08/1919	31/08/1919
War Diary		22/08/1919	07/09/1919
War Diary		05/09/1919	16/09/1919
War Diary	Berg-Gladbach	31/10/1919	31/10/1919
War Diary	Paffrath	31/10/1919	31/10/1919
War Diary	Berg-Gladbach	10/10/1919	31/10/1919

WO 95/22924

Dusronal Ammunition Column

29TH DIVISION
DIVL ARTILLERY

29TH DIVL AMMN COLUMN

MAR 1916 — ~~[illegible]~~

Oct 1919

Originally 53rd (Welch) Divisional A.C.

29th DIVISIONAL AMMUNITION COLUMN

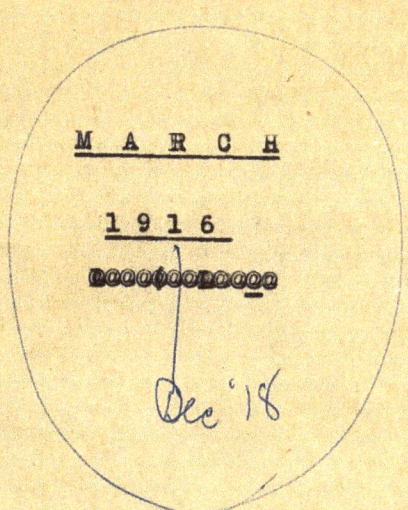

MARCH

1916

Dec '18

G.H.Q.

Confidential

War Diary

29 Division Ammn Col.
53rd (Welsh) Div'l Ammn. Col. LATE

From March 1st 1916 to March 31st 1916

Volume 3/1916

Army Form C. 2118

WAR DIARY
or
INTELLIGENCE SUMMARY
(Erase heading not required.)

Instructions regarding War Diaries and Intelligence Summaries are contained in F. S. Regs., Part II. and the Staff Manual respectively. Title Pages will be prepared in manuscript.

Place	Date	Hour	Summary of Events and Information	Remarks and references to Appendices
REBECQ.	1/3/16		Unit stationed at REBECQ, PAS-DE-CALAIS.	
do	24/3/16	9 AM	Unit moved by road.	
BERGENEUSE	do	5:30 PM	Unit arrived at BERGENEUSE where it billeted for the night.	
do	25/3/16	8 AM	Unit left by road via St POL.	
BONNIERES	do	5 PM	Unit arrived at BONNIERES where it billeted for the night.	
do	26/3/16	9 AM	Moved via DOULLENS	
TALMAS.	do	4 PM	Arrived at TALMAS & stayed till morning of 28th inst.	
do	28/3/16	9 AM	Left for CAUMESNIL.	
CAUMESNIL	do	4 PM	Arrived at CAUMESNIL & stayed until 31st inst.	
do	31/3/16	1 PM	Left for ARQUÈVES.	
ARQUÈVES	do	4 PM	Arrived at ARQUÈVES.	

H.V. Stocked Capt.
Adjutant.
33 WELSH DIVISIONAL AMMUNITION COLUMN.

29th DIVISIONAL AMMUNITION COLUMN

APRIL 1 9 1 6

Confidential

War Diary

of

29th Divisional Amm. Col.
late 53 (Welsh) Divl A.C.

from April 1st 1916 to April 30th 1916

Volume 1916

Army Form C. 2118

WAR DIARY
INTELLIGENCE SUMMARY
(Erase heading not required.)

Instructions regarding War Diaries and Intelligence Summaries are contained in F.S. Regs., Part II. and the Staff Manual respectively. Title Pages will be prepared in manuscript.

Place	Date	Hour	Summary of Events and Information	Remarks and references to Appendices
ARQUÈVES	1/4/16	—	Unit stationed at ARQUÈVES.	
"	9/4/16	—	Title of unit changed from 53 (Welsh) Divl Amm. Col. to 29th Divl Amm. Col. [No 1 Section still acting as 31st Divl Amm. Col.]	
"	19/4/16	—	No 1 Section rejoined this unit for duty.	

29th DIVISIONAL AMMUNITION COLUMN

MAY 1916

29 Dec Am Cal.
Vol 5

War Diary
Div... 1/1/16 - 31/5/16

WAR DIARY or INTELLIGENCE SUMMARY

Army Form C. 2118

HEADQUARTERS, 29th DIVISIONAL AMMUNITION COLUMN.

Place	Date	Hour	Summary of Events and Information	Remarks and references to Appendices
ARQUEVES	1/5/16	—	Unit Stationed at Arqueves.	
"	13/5/16	—	Reconstruction of Unit. No. 1, 2 & 3 Sections also all Ranks were formed into No 4 Section "B" Echelon S.G.R.D.A.C. remainder of Officers & men of 1, 2, & 3 Sections becoming supplies. A. Echelon of this Unit being formed from 15th B.A.C. R.H.A. becoming No 1 Section, 17th B.A.C. becoming No 2 Section & 14th B.A.C. becoming No 3 Section. The Personnel of 132nd B.A.C. Sixteen being absorbed by the three new Sections Brigades.	
"	25/5/16	—	H.Q.S. moved from Arqueves to Amplier	
"	26/5/16	—	No 3 Section have from Arqueves to Acheux. No 1 Section moved from Arqueves to Amplier	
AMPLIER	31/5/16	—	H.Q.S. Stationed at Amplier	
"	"		No 1 & 4 Sections Stationed at Amplier	
"	"		No 2 & 3 Sections Stationed at Acheux	

Lieut. Colonel,
COMDG. 29th DIVISIONAL AMMUNITION COLUMN.

29th DIVISIONAL AMMUNITION COLUMN

JUNE 1916

Army Form C. 2118

WAR DIARY
or
INTELLIGENCE SUMMARY

(Erase heading not required.)

Du Aux Cat
Vol 6

Place	Date	Hour	Summary of Events and Information	Remarks and references to Appendices
AMPLIER	1-6-16		Headquarters and No's 1 & 4 Sections Stationed at AMPLIER	
"	1-6-16		No's 2 & 3 Sections Stationed at ACHEUX	
"	17-6-16		No. 1 Section moved to ACHEUX	
ACHEUX	20-6-16		Headquarters moved to ACHEUX	
ACHEUX	30-6-16		Headquarters and No's 1, 2, & 3 Sections stationed at ACHEUX	
"	30-6-16		No 4 Section stationed at AMPLIER	

H.B.Tooker.
Capt. R.A.M.C.
for / LIEUT. COLONEL
COMDG. 29th DIVISIONAL F. STN COLUMN.

29th DIVISIONAL AMMUNITION COLUMN

JULY 1916

Army Form C. 2118

29D Am Col

Vol VII

WAR DIARY
or
INTELLIGENCE SUMMARY
(Erase heading not required.)

Instructions regarding War Diaries and Intelligence Summaries are contained in F.S. Regs., Part II. and the Staff Manual respectively. Title Pages will be prepared in manuscript.

Place	Date	Hour	Summary of Events and Information	Remarks and references to Appendices
ACHEUX	1-7-16		Headquarters and Nos 1, 2 & 3 Sections stationed at ACHEUX.	
"	"		No 4 Section stationed at AMPLIER.	
"	"		No 1 Section moved to ENGLEBELMER	
AMPLIER	6/7/16		Headquarters & Nos 1 & 2 Sections moved to AMPLIER	
"	20/7/16		No 3 Section moved from ACHEUX to AMPLIER	
"	"		No 1 Section moved from AMPLIER to ACHEUX	
"	27/7/16		No 1 Section moved from ACHEUX to BERTRANCOURT	
"	28/7/16		The Small Arms Ammunition sections of Nos 1, 2, 3 & 4 Sections organised into "A" "B" & "C"	
"	"		S.A.A. Subsections entrained and departed as under:-	
"	"	8.19am	"A" consisting of 1 Officer 60 other ranks 98 animals & 19 vehicles from DOULLENS N.	
"	"	9.4	"B" consisting of 1 Officer 62 other ranks 100 animals & 20 vehicles from DOULLENS S.	
"	"	9.36	"C" consisting of 1 Officer 61 other ranks 99 animals & 20 vehicles from CANDAS	
AMPLIER	31-7-16		Headquarters No 2, 3 & 4 Sections stationed at AMPLIER	
			No 1 Section stationed at BERTRANCOURT	

ADJUTANT,
29 DIVISIONAL AMMUNITION COLUMN.

29th DIVISIONAL AMMUNITION COLUMN

AUGUST 1 9 1 6

29th D.A.C.

Army Form C. 2118

WAR DIARY
or
INTELLIGENCE SUMMARY
(Erase heading not required.)

29 D.A.C. Vol 5 Pt 1

Place	Date	Hour	Summary of Events and Information	Remarks and references to Appendices
AMPLIER	1/8/16		Headquarters, No 2, 3 & 4 Sections stationed at AMPLIER. No 1 Section stationed at BERTRANCOURT	
	6/8/16		No 1 Section moved from BERTRANCOURT to ACHEUX	
	8/8/16		1 Officer & 30 Other ranks entrained at DOULLENS to proceed to join S.A.A. Section attached to 20th D.A.C.	
	9/8/16		No 2 Section moved from AMPLIER to ACHEUX	
ACHEUX	10/8/16		Headquarters moved from AMPLIER to ACHEUX	
	14/8/16		No 3 & 4 Sections moved from AMPLIER to ACHEUX	
	17/8/16		Personnel of S/29, V/29, X/29, Y/29, & Z/29 Trench Mortar Batteries transferred to this Unit (Authority A.G. No 1055/16 d) 9/8/16)	
	31/8/16		Headquarters Nos 1, 2, 3 & 4 Sections stationed at ACHEUX	

St Rue Dunn
LIEUT. COLONEL
29 DIVISION AMMUNITION COLUMN

29th DIVISIONAL AMMUNITION COLUMN

SEPTEMBER 1916

CONFIDENTIAL

WAR DIARY

OF

29TH. DIVISIONAL AMMN. COLUMN

FROM 1-9-16 TO 30-9-16

VOLUME 5

Army Form C. 2118

WAR DIARY
or
INTELLIGENCE SUMMARY
(Erase heading not required.)

Instructions regarding War Diaries and Intelligence Summaries are contained in F. S. Regs., Part II. and the Staff Manual respectively. Title Pages will be prepared in manuscript.

Place	Date	Hour	Summary of Events and Information	Remarks and references to Appendices
ACHEUX	1/9/16		Headquarters Nos 1, 2, 3 Y 4 Sections stationed at ACHEUX	
	7/9/16		Headquarters Nos 1, 2, 3 Y 4 Sections moved from ACHEUX to ORVILLE	
	8/9/16		Headquarters No 1, 2, 3 Y 4 Sections moved from ORVILLE to VACQUERIE-LE-BOUCQ	
	9/9/16		Headquarters Nos 3 Y 4 Sections moved from VACQUERIE-LE-BOUCQ to WAVRANS Nos 1 Y 2 Sections moved from VACQUERIE-LE-BOUCQ to FLEURY	
	10/9/16		Headquarters Nos 3 Y 4 Sections moved from WAVRANS to ENGUINEGATTE Nos 1 Y 2 Sections moved from FLEURY to ENGUINEGATTE	
	11/9/16		Headquarters Nos 1, 2, 3 Y 4 Sections moved from ENGUINEGATTE to NORDPEENE	
	12/9/16		Headquarters Nos 1, 2, 3 Y 4 Sections moved from NORDPEENE to POPERINGHE S.A.A. Subsection of Nos 1, 2, 3 Y 4 Sections rejoined their respective Sections	
POPERINGHE	13/9/16 30/9/16		Headquarters Nos 1, 2, 3 Y 4 Sections stationed at POPERINGHE	

S.D. McEvans
LIEUT. COLONEL
COMDG. 29 DIVISIONAL AMMUNITION COLUMN.

29th DIVISIONAL AMMUNITION COLUMN

OCTOBER 1 9 1 6

29th DIVISIONAL AMMUNITION COLUMN

Vol 10

CONFIDENTIAL

— WAR DIARY —

OF

29th Divisional Ammunition Column

from 1st October 1916 to 31st October 1916

(Volume 6)

Army Form C. 2118

WAR DIARY
or
INTELLIGENCE SUMMARY
(Erase heading not required.)

Instructions regarding War Diaries and Intelligence Summaries are contained in F.S. Regs., Part II. and the Staff Manual respectively. Title Pages will be prepared in manuscript.

Place	Date	Hour	Summary of Events and Information	Remarks and references to Appendices
POPERINCHE	1/10/16		Headquarters Nos 1, 2, 3, 4 Sections stationed at POPERINGHE	JWR
HERZEELE	8/10/16		Headquarters Nos 1, 3 & 4 Sections moved from POPERINCHE to HERZEELE	JWR
			No 2 Section moved from POPERINGHE to WORMHOUDT	
"	10/10/16		A portion of Nos 1, 2, 3 & 4 Sections moved to and entrained at HOPOUTRE	
			Headquarters, remaining portion of No 1 Section & another portion of No 4 Section moved to and entrained at PROVEN	
			Remaining portion of Nos 2, 3 & 4 Sections moved to and entrained at ESQUEBEC	JWR
DAOURS	11/10/16		Headquarters No 1 Section and portion of Nos 2, 3 & 4 Sections detrained at SALEUX and proceeded to DAOURS	JWR
			Remaining portion of Nos 2, 3 & 4 Sections detrained at LONGUEAU and proceeded to DAOURS	JWR
	12/10/16		Headquarters Nos 1, 2, 3 & 4 Sections proceeded from DAOURS to BUIRE	JWR
BAZENTIN-LE-GRAND	14/10/16		Headquarters Nos 1, 2, 3 & 4 Sections (also S.A.A. Section) moved from BUIRE to BAZENTIN-LE-GRAND	JWR
"	18/10/16		S.A.A. Section (consisting of 7 Officers 238 OR 31 Riding Horses 81 Draught and 22 pack 43 G.S. Wagons 15 Limbered G.S. Wagons Water Cart & Mess Cart & 3 Bicycles) moved from BUIRE to POMMIERS CAMP	JWR
	30/10/16		S.A.A Section moved from POMMIERS CAMP to ALBERT	JWR
	31/10/16		Headquarters Nos 1, 2, 3 & 4 Sections (also S.A.A Sections) stationed at BAZENTIN-LE-GRAND	JWR
			S.A.A. Section stationed at ALBERT	JWR

Wm Smith
LIEUT. COLONEL.
COMDG. 29 DIVISIONAL AMMUNITION COLUMN

29th DIVISIONAL AMMUNTTION COLUMN

NOVEMBER 1 9 1 6

Vol XI

CONFIDENTIAL

WAR DIARY

OF

29th Divisional Ammunition Column

from 1st Nov 1916 to 30th Nov 1916

(Volume No 7)

Army Form C. 2118

WAR DIARY
or
INTELLIGENCE SUMMARY
(Erase heading not required.)

Instructions regarding War Diaries and Intelligence Summaries are contained in F. S. Regs., Part II. and the Staff Manual respectively. Title Pages will be prepared in manuscript.

Place	Date	Hour	Summary of Events and Information	Remarks and references to Appendices
BAZENTIN LE-GRAND	1/11/16		Headquarters Nos 1, 2, 3 & 4 Sections (less A.A.A. Section) stationed at BAZENTIN LE-GRAND	AR
MEAULTE	26/11/16		Headquarters Nos 1, 2, 3 & 4 Sections (less A.A.A. Section) moved from BAZENTIN LE-GRAND to Cavalry Camp MEAULTE	AR
CARNOY	29/11/16		Headquarters No 1, 3 & 4 Sections (less A.A.A. Section) moved from MEAULTE to CARNOY. No 2 A.A.A. Section rejoined No 2 Section at Cavalry Camp MEAULTE. Remaining portion of A.A.A. Section rejoined Nos 1, 3 & 4 Sections at CARNOY	3AR
	30/11/16		Headquarters Nos 1, 3, & 4 Sections stationed at CARNOY. No 2 Section stationed at Cavalry Camp MEAULTE	3AR

Harold Phelan Lt Col
for LIEUT COLONEL
COMDG. 29 DIVISIONAL AMMUNITION COLUMN.

WAR DIARY
or
INTELLIGENCE SUMMARY

(Erase heading not required.)

Army Form C. 2118

Instructions regarding War Diaries and Intelligence Summaries are contained in F.S. Regs., Part II and the Staff Manual respectively. Title Pages will be prepared in manuscript.

Place	Date	Hour	Summary of Events and Information	Remarks and references to Appendices
ALBERT.	1-11-1916	0900	No's 1, 2 & 4 Sections moved to CORBIE and were billeted in RUE du CHAVATIERS in ETAPLES-SUR-CORBIE. No 3 Section, recently commanded of Lieut G.R.B. NELSON, TF&A remained at ALBERT.	
CORBIE.	2-11-1916		21 G/S Wagons were employed on various Fatigues & similar orders from 29th Division	
	3-11-1916		14 G/S Wagons were employed on Fatigues & similar orders from D.H.Q. No 3 Section	
			29th Div. S.A.A. Column; never carried out by Lieut G.R.B. NELSON, TF&A, proceeded up to Corbie and were billeted in the same area as the rest of the Coy.	
	4-11-1916		6 Wagons were employed in Divisional Fatigues. 2 Lieut H Brodie, R.A. joined on recall to France & England.	
	5-11-1916		6 Wagons were employed on Divisional Fatigues	
	6-11-1916		8 " " " " " Lieut G.R.B. NELSON, TF&A, proceeded on his way to France & England. 1 Driver returned from sick leave in England.	
	7-11-1916		9 G/S Wagons were employed on Divisional Fatigues	
	8-11-1916		11 G/S Wagons " " " " " The S.A.A. Column was inspected by the Col of Command (Lieut-Col S.R. QUIN-DAVIS, TF&A.) in Drill Order (dismounted).	
	9-11-1916		6 G/S Wagons were employed on Divisional Fatigues. Lieut A Dalziel & 2 Lieut A.W. Dale, R.F.A. posted to 60th Divisional Artillery. 1 Driver returned to duty from Hospital.	

A.W. Date

WAR DIARY or INTELLIGENCE SUMMARY

Army Form C. 2118

(Erase heading not required.)

Instructions regarding War Diaries and Intelligence Summaries are contained in F.S. Regs., Part II. and the Staff Manual respectively. Title Pages will be prepared in manuscript.

Place	Date	Hour	Summary of Events and Information	Remarks and references to Appendices
CORBIE	10-11-16		10. G.S. Wagons were employed on Divisional Fatigues. 1 went Relieved L and L from Hospital. Rfmt G.H. Barber R.F.A. was posted from 183 Section 29th F.S.A.C. Section.	
	11-11-16		6. G.S. Wagons were employed on Divisional Fatigues. 1 man Returned to duty from Hospital.	
	12-11-16		16. G.S. Wagons were employed on Divisional Fatigues.	
	13-11-16		29. G.S. Wagons were employed on Divisional Fatigues. 1 man Returned to duty from Hospital.	
	14-11-16		24. G.S. Wagons were employed on Divisional Fatigues.	
	15-11-16		No. 3 Section 29th Div. S.A.A. Column moved on from CORBIE en route to Square S.W. Central of Licorn BERNAFAY and TRONES WOODS. We carried what is usually known as J. Infantry. G.H. Barber R.F.A. went to employ from J. Infantry ammunition. employed Wagons were by means of J. Infantry. G.S. Wagons and pack mules, & I. Infantry Javery Infantry employed as we moved. Fatigues. En L. Dennison. Some G.S. Wagons were attached to 80th Infantry Brigade and took to K 87th Infantry Bygnav. We moved off at 9.30. Column was under orders to move to CARNOY. No Section drew Rations and amounts of equipment etc. We packed amounts from the Section.	
	16-11-16		We 1 Section of N. 3 S.A.A. Column marched from CORBIE to Square F.9.5.6. meet CARNOY and billeted in 8th Bart. S.H. Column. Captain R.M. Dennison O.R.C. continued 6 Squares. S.Sap Carried ammunition and sent to 3rd Section and him change. was Section bivouacked in night at ALBERT.	
CARNOY	17-11-16		No 6 Squares of No. 3 Div.	
	18-11-16		20 G.S. Wagons were sent to the Senior Supply Officer to assist our Divisional Train from Railhead.	

Army Form C. 2118

WAR DIARY
or
INTELLIGENCE SUMMARY
(Erase heading not required.)

Instructions regarding War Diaries and Intelligence Summaries are contained in F.S. Regs., Part II. and the Staff Manual respectively. Title Pages will be prepared in manuscript.

Place	Date	Hour	Summary of Events and Information	Remarks and references to Appendices
Camp nr. CARNOY.	19-11-16		7 wagons were employed on Fatigues	
	20-11-16		17 " " " " " 15 men sent 12 miles from H.Qrs 29th D.A.C.	
	21-11-16		17 " " " " " Bext B.A.S. X.R. Fence returned from leave.	
	22-11-16		28 " " " " "	
	23-11-16		22 " " " " " 2d/Lt Griffiths was taken at GINCHY CORNER by a piece of H.E. and go to base to Hospital. 2d Lt Aldous posted for duty.	
	24-11-16		20 " " " " "	
	25-11-16		23 " " " " "	
	26-11-16		30 " " " " "	
	27-11-16		24 " " " " " 4 men posted from 29th T.M.B.	
	28-11-16		30 " " " " " 2/Lieut Norris posted to No1 Section 29th D.A.C.	
	29-11-16		29 " " " " " The Small Arms Sections now ceased to exist. The Small Arms Sections of Nº 1, 2 & 3 were returned to their respective Sections & S.A.A. on hand between the G.S. Wagons, Limbers and personnel of the four Sections of No4. The Section now re-becomes the original N.Q. of Nº4 Section, 29th Divl. Small Ammunition Column No 1-4.	

C.B.Negus
2/Lieut R.F.A.
for Captain R.H.A.
Commanding No4. Section, 29 D.A.C.

1875 Wt. W.593/826 1,000,000 4/15 J.B.C. & A. A.D.S.S./Forms/C. 2118.

29th DIVISIONAL AMMUNITION COLUMN

DECEMBER 1 9 1 6

CONFIDENTIAL

WAR DIARY

of

29th Divisional Ammunition Column

From 1st December 1916 To 31st December 1916

(Volume 8)

WAR DIARY
or
INTELLIGENCE SUMMARY

(Erase heading not required.)

Army Form C. 2118

Place	Date	Hour	Summary of Events and Information	Remarks and references to Appendices
CARNOY	1/12/16		Headquarters No 1 3 & 4 Sections stationed at CARNOY	
			No 2 Section stationed at Cavalry Camp MEAULTE	
	14/12/16		No 2 Section moved from MEAULTE to MORLANCOURT	
	28/12/16		No 2 Section moved from MORLANCOURT to CARNOY	
			No 1 Section moved from CARNOY to MORLANCOURT	
CARNOY	31/12/16		Headquarters No 2 3 & 4 Sections stationed at CARNOY	
			No 1 Section stationed at MORLANCOURT	

LIEUT. COLONEL.
COMDG. 29 DIVISIONAL AMMUNITION COLUMN.

Vol 13

CONFIDENTIAL

WAR DIARY

OF

29th Divisional Ammunition Column

From 1st January 1917 to 31st January 1917

(Volume 9)

Army Form C. 2118.

WAR DIARY
or
INTELLIGENCE SUMMARY.
(Erase heading not required.)

Instructions regarding War Diaries and Intelligence Summaries are contained in F. S. Regs., Part II. and the Staff Manual respectively. Title pages will be prepared in manuscript.

Place	Date	Hour	Summary of Events and Information	Remarks and references to Appendices
CARNOY	1/1/17		Headquarters, Nos 2, 3 & 4 Sections stationed at CARNOY	
	14/1/17		No 1 Section stationed at MORLANCOURT	
			No 1 Section moved from MORLANCOURT to CARNOY	
			No 3 Section moved from CARNOY to MORLANCOURT	
	18/1/17		No 3 Section became Ammunition Column 147 Brigade R.F.A. in lines of S.H.Q. No O.B. 1866 a/21/12/16	
	31/1/17		Headquarters No 1, 2 & 4 Sections stationed at CARNOY	

L. Price Davis
LIEUT COLONEL.
COMDG. 29 DIVISIONAL AMMUNITION COLUMN.

CONFIDENTIAL

WAR DIARY

OF

29th Divisional Ammunition Column

From 1st February 1917 to 28th February 1917

(Volume 10)

Army Form C. 2118.

WAR DIARY
or
INTELLIGENCE SUMMARY.
(Erase heading not required.)

Place	Date	Hour	Summary of Events and Information	Remarks and references to Appendices
CARNOY	1/2/17		Headquarters Nos 1, 2 & 4 Sections stationed at CARNOY	
"	12/2/17		Draft of One Officer and 114 other ranks arrived from Base	
"	21/2/17		Draft of 32 other ranks arrived from Base	
"	28/2/17		Headquarters Nos 1, 2 & 4 Sections stationed at CARNOY	

Howard Rich Lt/Adjt
for LIEUT. COLONEL
Comdg. 29 Divisional Ammunition Column.

Vol 15

CONFIDENTIAL

WAR DIARY

OF

29th Divisional Ammunition Column

From 1st March 1917 to 31st March 1917

(Volume 11)

Army Form C. 2118.

WAR DIARY
or
INTELLIGENCE SUMMARY.
(Erase heading not required.)

Place	Date	Hour	Summary of Events and Information	Remarks and references to Appendices
CARNOY	1/3/17		Headquarters No 1, 2 Y 3 Sections stationed at CARNOY	
MORLANCOURT	21/3/17		Headquarters No 1, 2 Y 3 Sections moved from CARNOY to MORLANCOURT	
LA HOUSSOYE	23/3/17		Headquarters No 1 Y 2 Sections moved from MORLANCOURT to LA HOUSSOYE. No 3 Section remained at MORLANCOURT as staff section	
HAVERNAS	24/3/17		Headquarters No 1 Y 2 Sections moved from LA HOUSSOYE to HAVERNAS	
BEAUVOIR RIVIERE	26/3/17		Headquarters No 1 Y 2 Sections moved from HAVERNAS to BEAUVOIR - RIVIERE	
GRAND BOURET	27/3/17		Headquarters No 1 Y 2 Sections moved from BEAUVOIR RIVIERE to GRAND BOURET	
GOUVES	28/3/17		Headquarters No 1 Y 2 Sections moved from GRAND BOURET to GOUVES	
	31/3/17		Headquarters No 1 Y 2 Sections stationed at GOUVES	

Harold Rhodes Lieut
LIEUT. COLONEL
COMDG. 29 DIVISIONAL AMBULANCE COLUMN.

Vol 16

CONFIDENTIAL

WAR DIARY

OF

29th Divl Ammunition Column

From 1st April 1917 to 31st April 1917

(Volume II)

Army Form C. 2118.

WAR DIARY
or
INTELLIGENCE SUMMARY.
(Erase heading not required.)

Place	Date	Hour	Summary of Events and Information	Remarks and references to Appendices
GOUVES	1/4/17		Headquarters No 1 & 2 Sections stationed at GOUVES No 3 Section on detachment as Still Sections under 29th Division Q	
"	8/4/17		"A" Echelon Gun Section moved from GOUVES to ARRAS	
"	11/4/17		Headquarters and B Echelon Gun Section moved from GOUVES to ARRAS	
ARRAS	30/4/17		Headquarters No 1 & 2 Sections stationed at ARRAS	

James Rutherford
Lieut. Colonel.
Comdg. 29 Divisional Ammunition Column.

CONFIDENTIAL

WAR DIARY
OF
29th DIVISIONAL AMMUNITION COLUMN

FROM 1-5-17 to 31-5-17

(VOLUME NO 13)

Army Form C. 2118.

WAR DIARY
or
INTELLIGENCE SUMMARY.
(Erase heading not required.)

Instructions regarding War Diaries and Intelligence Summaries are contained in F.S. Regs., Part II. and the Staff Manual respectively. Title pages will be prepared in manuscript.

Place	Date	Hour	Summary of Events and Information	Remarks and references to Appendices
ARRAS	1-5-17		Headquarters Nos 1 & 2 Sections stationed at ARRAS	
"	"		No 3 Section on detachment as S.A.A Section under 29th Division G	
"	19-8-17		No 3 Section rejoined Column	
"	21-8-17		Headquarters Nos 1, 2 & 3 Sections stationed at ARRAS	

[signature]

LIEUT. COLONEL.
COMDG. 29th DIVISIONAL AMMUNITION COLUMN.

CONFIDENTIAL

WAR DIARY

OF

29th Divisional Ammn Column

From 1-6-17   To 30-6-17

VOLUME 14

Army Form C. 2118.

WAR DIARY
or
INTELLIGENCE SUMMARY.
(Erase heading not required.)

Instructions regarding War Diaries and Intelligence Summaries are contained in F.S. Regs., Part II. and the Staff Manual respectively. Title pages will be prepared in manuscript.

Place	Date	Hour	Summary of Events and Information	Remarks and references to Appendices
ARRAS	1.6.17		Headquarters Nos 1, 2, & 3 Sections stationed at ARRAS	WR.
"	3.6.17		No 3 Section on detachment as a.a. Section under 29th Division @	WR.
"	22.6.17		Headquarters Nos 1 & 2 Sections moved to GOUVES	WR.
"	30.6.17		Headquarters Nos 1 & 2 Sections stationed at GOUVES	WR.

Harold Rhodes Lewis
for LIEUT. COLONEL.
COMDG. 29th DIVISIONAL AMMUNITION COLUMN.

CONFIDENTIAL

WAR DIARY

OF

29th Divisional Ammunition Column.

From 1-7-17 To 31-7-17.

(VOLUME XV)

Army Form C. 2118.

WAR DIARY
or
INTELLIGENCE SUMMARY.
(Erase heading not required.)

Instructions regarding War Diaries and Intelligence Summaries are contained in F. S. Regs., Part II. and the Staff Manual respectively. Title pages will be prepared in manuscript.

Place	Date	Hour	Summary of Events and Information	Remarks and references to Appendices
GOUVES	1-7-17	11.30 a.m.	Headquarters Nos 1 and 2 Sections stationed at GOUVES.	AR
"	1-7-17	12 noon	" " " " moved to ETREE WAMIN	AR
ETREE WAMIN	2-7-17		" " " " " CROIX.	AR
CROIX	3-7-17		" " " " stationed at CROIX	AR
"	4-7-17		" " " " moved to NEDON & NEDONCHELLE	AR
NEDON & NEDONCHELLE NEUFPRE Environs of AIRE	5-7-17		" " " " " NEUFPRE & Environs of AIRE	AR
"	6-7-17		" " " " " STAPLE	AR
STAPLE	7-7-17		" " " " " GODEWAERSVELDE	AR
GODEWAERS VELDE	8-7-17		" " " " " INTERNATIONAL CORNER near PESELHOEK	AR
	9-7-17		" " " " stationed at { INTERNATIONAL CORNER	
	31-7-17		" " " " " NEAR PESELHOEK.	AR.

Howard Plnden
LIEUT. COLONEL.
COMDG. 29 DIVISIONAL AMMUNITION COLUMN.

Vol 22

CONFIDENTIAL

WAR DIARY

OF

29th DIVL. AMMUNITION COLUMN

(VOLUME No 18)

CONFIDENTIAL

WAR DIARY

OF

29th Divl Ammn Column

From 1/8/1 to 31/8/1

(VOLUME No. 16)

Army Form C. 2118

WAR DIARY
or
INTELLIGENCE SUMMARY

(Erase heading not required.)

Instructions regarding War Diaries and Intelligence Summaries are contained in F. S. Regs., Part II. and the Staff Manual respectively. Title Pages will be prepared in manuscript.

Place	Date	Hour	Summary of Events and Information	Remarks and references to Appendices
INTERNATIONAL CORNER	1/8/17		Headquarters Nos 1 & 2 Sections stationed at INTERNATIONAL CORNER near PESEL HOEK	
"	14/8/17		Headquarters Nos 1 & 2 Sections moved to (B.7.d.2.3) near ELVERDINGHE.	
(B.7.d.2.3) N. ELVERDINGHE	31/8/17		Headquarters Nos 1, 2 Sections stationed at (B.7.d.2.3) near ELVERDINGHE	

J R Watson Lieut
for LIEUT. COLONEL,
COMDG. 29 DIVISIONAL AMMUNITION COLUMN.

CONFIDENTIAL

WAR DIARY

OF

29th Divisional Ammn Column

1-9-17   30-9-17

(VOLUME No 17)

Army Form C. 2118

WAR DIARY
or
INTELLIGENCE SUMMARY
(Erase heading not required.)

Instructions regarding War Diaries and Intelligence Summaries are contained in F. S. Regs., Part II. and the Staff Manual respectively. Title Pages will be prepared in manuscript.

17

Place	Date	Hour	Summary of Events and Information	Remarks and references to Appendices
(B, q, d 23) ELVERDINGHE	1.9.17		Headquarters Nos 1 and 2 Sections stationed at (B q d 23) near ELVERDINGHE	
"	12.9.17	11.30 PM	12 Right shaft Ammunition Rifles by Shell Fire	
"	"		2.0 " " Wounded	
"	"		No 3 Section re-joined Column	
"	22.9.17			
"	25.9.17	8.0 pm	One Other Rank Killed by Bombs dropped from Hostile Aircraft	
"	"		Three " " Wounded " " " "	
"	"		38 Right shaft Ammunition Rifles by Bombs dropped from Hostile Aircraft	
"	"		8 " " " Wounded " " " " " "	
(A 12) near ELVERDINGHE	30.9.17		Headquarters Nos 1, 2 and 3 Sections stationed at (A 12) near ELVERDINGHE	

Harold Rhodes, Captain
for LIEUT. COLONEL
COMDG. 29th DIVISIONAL AMMUNITION COLUMN

Army Form C. 2118

WAR DIARY
or
INTELLIGENCE SUMMARY
(Erase heading not required.)

Instructions regarding War Diaries and Intelligence Summaries are contained in F.S. Regs., Part II. and the Staff Manual respectively. Title Pages will be prepared in manuscript.

Place	Date	Hour	Summary of Events and Information	Remarks and references to Appendices
B.T. & 3 NEAR ELVERDINGHE	1/10/17		Headquarters Nos 1, 2 & 3 Sections stationed at (B.T. & 23) Near ELVERDINGHE	JAP
	10/10/17		Under authority delegated by His Majesty the King, the Field Marshal in Chief has awarded the DISTINGUISHED CONDUCT MEDAL to No 122596 Driver (A/Bm) J. P. Burford No 1 Section 29th Divl Amm Column	JAP
	24/10/17		Headquarters Nos 1, 2 & 3 Sections entrained for DOULLENS 25.10.17	JAP
DOULLENS	25/10/17		Headquarters Nos 1, 2 & 3 Sections marched to AMPLIER	JAP
AMPLIER	30/10/17		Headquarters Nos 1, 2 & 3 Sections stationed at AMPLIER	JAP

Isaac Rinden Capt.
for Lieut Colonel

Vol 23

CONFIDENTIAL

WAR DIARY

OF

29th DIVL AMM COLUMN

From 1-11-17 To 30-11-17

(VOLUME No 19).

Army Form C. 2118

WAR DIARY
or
INTELLIGENCE SUMMARY
(Erase heading not required.)

Instructions regarding War Diaries and Intelligence Summaries are contained in F. S. Regs., Part II. and the Staff Manual respectively. Title Pages will be prepared in manuscript.

Place	Date	Hour	Summary of Events and Information	Remarks and references to Appendices
AMPLIER	1-11-17		Headquarters Nos 1, 2, S.A.A. Sections stationed at AMPLIER	JR
"	7-11-17		S.A.A. Section moved to BRAYE	JR
"	8-11-17		" " " " Camp at V3C near EQUANCOURT	JR
"	12-11-17		Hqrs Nos 1 & 2 Sections moved to VILLE-SOUR-ANCRE	JR
VILLE-SOUR ANCRE	13-11-17		" " " " Stationed at VILLE-SOUR ANCRE	JR
"	14-11-17		Hqrs Nos 1 & 2 Sections moved to Camp at V3C near EQUANCOURT	JR
CAMP V C 3	30-11-17		Hqrs Nos 1, 2 & S.A.A. Sections stationed at Camp V 30 "	JR

James P. _____ Capt.

A/ LIEUT. COLONEL.
COMDG. 29 DIVISIONAL AMMUNITION COLUMN.

1875 Wt. W593/826 1,000,000 4/15 J.B.C. & A. A.D.S.S./Forms/C. 2118.

CONFIDENTIAL WAR DIARY

OF

29th DIVISIONAL AMMUNITION COLUMN

FROM 1-12-17   TO 31-12-17

VOLUME No. 20

WAR DIARY
or
INTELLIGENCE SUMMARY

(Erase heading not required.)

Army Form C. 2118

Instructions regarding War Diaries and Intelligence Summaries are contained in F. S. Regs., Part II. and the Staff Manual respectively. Title Pages will be prepared in manuscript.

Place	Date	Hour	Summary of Events and Information	Remarks and references to Appendices
CAMP V.C3 N'EQUANCOURT	11.12.17		Hqrs No 1, 2 + 3 Sections stationed at Camp V.C.3 NEW EQUANCOURT	See
	14.12.17		Hqrs Nos 1 + 3 Section moved to TREUX	See
			No 2 Section on detachment with 17 Brigade RFA	See
TREUX	19.12.17		Hqrs and No 3 Section moved to ACHEUX	See
			No 1 Section moved to LOUVENCOURT	See
			No 2 Section rejoined Column	See
ACHEUX	20.12.17		Hqrs Nos 1, 2 + 3 Sections moved to GAZAINCOURT	See
	21.12.17			
GAZAINCOURT	23.12.17		Hqrs Nos 2 + 3 Sections moved to AVERO METZ	See
			No 1 Section moved to ROUBERS Sur CANCHE	
	24.12.17		Hqrs and No 2 Section moved to OFFIN	See
			No 1 Section moved to HESMOND	
			No 3 Section moved to LOISON	
OFFIN	31.12.17		Hqrs and No 2 Section stationed at OFFIN	See
			No 1 Section stationed at HESMOND	
			No 3 Section stationed at LOISON	

Confidential

War Diary of

29th Divl Ammn Column

From 1/1/18 To 31/1/18

(Volume No 21)

Vol 25

Army Form C. 2118.

WAR DIARY
or
INTELLIGENCE SUMMARY.
(Erase heading not required.)

Instructions regarding War Diaries and Intelligence Summaries are contained in F. S. Regs., Part II. and the Staff Manual respectively. Title pages will be prepared in manuscript.

Place	Date	Hour	Summary of Events and Information	Remarks and references to Appendices
OFFIN	1-1-18		Headquarters & No. 2 Section stationed at OFFIN	JR
			No. 1 Section stationed at HESMOND	JR
			SAA Section " " LOISON	JR
	3-1-18		Headquarters, Nos 1, 2 & SAA Sections move to VERCHOCQ	JR
VERCHOCQ	4-1-18		Hqrs Nos 1 & 2 Sections moved to MERCK-ST-LIEVIN	JR
			SAA Section moved to LA BUCILLE & CLOQUANT	JR
MERCK ST LIEVIN	11-1-18		Headquarters Nos 1, 2 & SAA Sections moved to Area of RENESCURE	JR
RENESCURE	12-1-18		" " " " OUDEZEELE	JR
OUDEZEELE	13-1-18		" " " " BUSSEBOOM	JR
BUSSEBOOM	21-1-18		" " " " VLAMERTINGHE	JR
VLAMERTINGHE	31-1-18		Headquarters Nos 1, 2 & SAA Section stationed at VLAMERTINGHE	JR

Harold Rhodes Capt.
for Lieut Colonel,
29 Divisional Ammunition Column

Confidential

War Diary

of

29th Ind Amm Column

From 1-2-18   To 28-2-18

Volume No 22

Army Form C. 2118.

WAR DIARY
or
INTELLIGENCE SUMMARY.
(Erase heading not required.)

Place	Date	Hour	Summary of Events and Information	Remarks and references to Appendices
VLAMERTINGHE	1-2-18		Headquarters Nos 1, 2 & 3 S.A.A. Sections stationed at VLAMERTINGHE	
	14.2.18		Headquarters Nos 1, 2 & 3 S.A.A. Sections moved to Camps on POPERINGHE - ELVERDINGHE Road	
	28/2/18		Headquarters Nos 1, 2 & 3 S.A.A. Sections stationed at CAMPS on POPERINGHE - ELVERDINGHE Road	

Llewelyn
Lieut
for O.C. 29th Div Amm Column

Army Form C. 2118.

WAR DIARY
or
INTELLIGENCE SUMMARY.
(Erase heading not required.)

DAColumn

Vol 27

Place	Date	Hour	Summary of Events and Information	Remarks and references to Appendices
Headquarters	1-3-18		Nos 1, 2 and S.A.A. Sections stationed at Camps on POPERINGHE-ELVERDINGHE Road	
Headquarters	9-3-18		Nos 1, 2 and S.A.A. Sections moved to ROAD CAMP VLAMERTINGHE	
Headquarters	31-3-18		Nos 1, 2 and S.A.A. Sections stationed at ROAD CAMP, VLAMERTINGHE	

E Murphy Lt
R.F.A.
for O.C. 28th DIVISIONAL AMMUNITION COLUMN

29th Divisional Artillery.

29th DIVISIONAL AMMUNITION COLUMN R.F.A.

APRIL 1918.

CONFIDENTIAL

WAR DIARY

OF

29th DIV. AMM COLUMN

FROM 1-4-18 To 30-4-18

VOLUME No 24

Army Form C. 2118.

WAR DIARY
or
INTELLIGENCE SUMMARY.
(Erase heading not required.)

Instructions regarding War Diaries and Intelligence Summaries are contained in F. S. Regs., Part II. and the Staff Manual respectively. Title pages will be prepared in manuscript.

Place	Date	Hour	Summary of Events and Information	Remarks and references to Appendices
VLAMERTINGHE	1-4-18		Headquarters Nos 1, 2 and S.A.A. Section at Road Camp VLAMERTINGHE	
	10-4-18		S.A.A Section on attachment with 29th Division Q.	
	15-4-18		Headquarters Nos 1 and 2 Section moved from Road Camp VLAMERTINGHE to Camp on PEPERINGHE-ELVERDINGHE Road	
	25-4-18		Headquarters Nos 1 and 2 Section moved from Camp on PEPERINGHE-ELVERDINGHE Road to HAMHOEK	
HAMHOEK	30-4-18		Headquarters Nos 1 and 2 Section stationed at HAMHOEK	

James Kirby Capt
for O.C. 29th Divisional Ammunition Column

T2134. Wt. W708—776. 500000. 4/15. Sir J. C. & S.

Confidential

War Diary

of

29th Div. Ammunition Column

From 1/3/10 to 31/3/10

Volume No 25

Army Form C. 2118.

WAR DIARY
or
INTELLIGENCE SUMMARY.
(Erase heading not required.)

Instructions regarding War Diaries and Intelligence Summaries are contained in F. S. Regs., Part II. and the Staff Manual respectively. Title pages will be prepared in manuscript.

Place	Date	Hour	Summary of Events and Information	Remarks and references to Appendices
HAMMEK	1.5.18		No. 1 & 2 Sections stationed at HAMMEK.	AAA
	17.5.18		No. 1 & No. 1 & 2 Sections moved to camp at C.22.d.2.2 (Sheet 36A) near LYNDE	AAA
			No. 1 Section moved to LYNDE	AAA
	18.5.18		No. 2 Section moved to Camp at D.1.D.1.0 (Sheet 36A)	AAA
	20.5.18		No. 1 Section moved to camp at V.25.a.5.3 (Sheet 27)	AAA
	22.5.18		No. 2 Section moved to camp at C.3.d.2.5 (Sheet 32A) near SERCUS	AAA
	25.5.18		No. 1 & 2 Sections marched to SERCUS	AAA
	31.5.18		Staff Billeted at camp at C.3.d.2.5 (Sheet 32A) near SERCUS	AAA
	31.5.18		No. 1 & 2 Sections stationed at SERCUS	AAA

Harold Hardy 2/Lt
for LIEUT. COLONEL
9th Divisional Ammunition Column.

Confidential War Diary

29th Divisional Ammunition Column

from

June 1st 1918 to June 30th 1918

Volume No 26.

WAR DIARY or INTELLIGENCE SUMMARY.

(Erase heading not required.)

Army Form C. 2118.

Place	Date	Hour	Summary of Events and Information	Remarks and references to Appendices
SERCUS	1-6-16		Hdqrs stationed at camp at C.3.d.2.5. near SERCUS	
do	1-6-16		Nos 1 and 2 Sections stationed at SERCUS	
do	30-6-16		Hdqrs stationed at camp at C.3.d.2.5 near SERCUS	
do	30-6-16		Nos 1 and 2 Sections stationed at SERCUS	

OMKing Capt.
for OFFR I/C ORC.
29th DIVISIONAL AMMUNITION COLUMN.

Confidential

War Diary

of

29th Div Ammn Column

From 1/7/18 to 31/7/18

VOLUME No. 27

Army Form C. 2118.

WAR DIARY
or
INTELLIGENCE SUMMARY.
(Erase heading not required.)

Instructions regarding War Diaries and Intelligence Summaries are contained in F. S. Regs., Part II. and the Staff Manual respectively. Title pages will be prepared in manuscript.

Place	Date	Hour	Summary of Events and Information	Remarks and references to Appendices
SERCUS	1/7/18		Hqrs Stationed at Camp at C.3.2.25 near SERCUS	
			Nos 1 & 2 Sections Stationed at SERCUS	
A.23.2.69	25/7/18		Hqrs Nos 1 & 2 Sections moved to Camp at A.23.2.69 near LA SABLIÈRE	
	22/7/18		S.A.A. Section rejoined Column 22-7-18	
			Hqrs Nos 1, 2 and S.A.A Section moved to Camp at COIN PERDU	
COIN PERDU	26/7/18		Nos 1 & Section moved to at LYNDE ST SYLVESTRE CAPPEL	
"	30/7/18		No 1 Section rejoined Column at COIN PERDU	
"	31/7/18		Headquarters Nos 1, 2 and S.A.A Section stationed at COIN PERDU	

Harold Pugh
for LIEUT. COLONEL Captain
COMDG. 29th Divisional Ammunition Column

T.134. Wt. W708—776. 500000. 4/15. Sir J. C. & S.

Confidential

War Diary

of

29th Divisional Ammunition Column

From 1/8/18 To 31/8/18

Volume No 28

Army Form C. 2118.

WAR DIARY
or
INTELLIGENCE SUMMARY.
(Erase heading not required.)

Instructions regarding War Diaries and Intelligence Summaries are contained in F.S. Regs., Part II. and the Staff Manual respectively. Title pages will be prepared in manuscript.

Place	Date	Hour	Summary of Events and Information	Remarks and references to Appendices
COIN PERDU	1-8-18		Headquarters Nos. 1, 2 and S.A.A. Sections Stations at COIN PERDU.	HERb
	3-8-18		Headquarters moved to Camp at V.I.C.7.4 near HONDEGHEM.	RRb
"			No 1 Section " " " V.I.C.7.4 "	
"			No 2 Section " " " V.I.C.2.4 "	
"			S.A.A. Section " " " U.6.B.8.2 "	
	31-8-13		Headquarters Stations at Camp at V.I.C.7.4 "	RRRb
"			No 1 Section " " " V.I.C.7.4 "	
"			No 2 Section " " " V.I.C.2.4 "	
"			S.A.A. Section " " " U.6.B.8.2 "	

RRRobb Lieut
for LIEUT. COLONEL
COMDG. 29 DIVISIONAL AMMUNITION COLUMN.

T2134. Wt. W708—776. 500000. 4/15. Sir J. C. & S.

Vol 33

Confidential

War Diary

of

29th Divisional Ammunition Column

1-9-18 to 30-9-18.

Volume 29.

Army Form C. 2118.

Instructions regarding War Diaries and Intelligence Summaries are contained in F. S. Regs., Part II. and the Staff Manual respectively. Title pages will be prepared in manuscript.

WAR DIARY
or
INTELLIGENCE SUMMARY.
(Erase heading not required.)

Place	Date	Hour	Summary of Events and Information	Remarks and references to Appendices
Near HONDEGHAM	1-9-18		Headquarters moved to Comb at 27/ W.13.D.6.2	
"	"		No 1 Section " " W.21.C.3.6	
"	"		No 2 Section " " W.14.a.8.8	
"	"		S.A.A Section " " V.18.D.8.8.	
"	3-9-18		S.A.A Section " " X.8.Central	
"	12-9-18		S.A.A Section " " V.18.D.8.8.	
"	16-9-18		Headquarters moved " " E.26.a.5.3.	
"	"		No 1 Section " " E.27.D.8.8.	
"	"		No 2 Section " " E.27.c.3.3	
"	19-9-18		S.A.A Section " " 287 K.8.G.2.2.	
"	21-9-18		S.A.A Section " " H.2.D.6.5	
"	27.9.18		Headquarters " " A.28.a.27	
"	"		No 1 Section " " G.3.b.4.5	
"	"		No 2 Section " " A.21.G.2.9.	
"	28-9-18		No 1 Section " " I.9.C.1.8	
"	"		S.A.A Section " " I.9.D.7.0.	

T2134. Wt. W708–776. 500000. 4/15. Sir J. C. & S.

Army Form C. 2118.

WAR DIARY
or
INTELLIGENCE SUMMARY.
(Erase heading not required.)

Instructions regarding War Diaries and Intelligence Summaries are contained in F. S. Regs., Part II. and the Staff Manual respectively. Title pages will be prepared in manuscript.

Place	Date	Hour	Summary of Events and Information	Remarks and references to Appendices
	29.9.18		Headquarters moved to 28/I.9.c.7.6.	
	"		No 2 Section to I.16.c.6.8.	
	30.9.18		Headquarters stationed at I.9.c.7.6.	
	"		No 1 Section " I.9.3.1.8	
	"		No 2 Section " I.16.c.6.8	
	"		S.A.A. Section " I.9.2.7.0.	

Howard Ricks
Capt
For Lieut. Compt
29-9-18 Division Ammunition Column

B de Mayn

Confidential

War Diary

of

29th Divisional Amm Column

1/10/18 to 31/10/18

Volume No 30

Army Form C. 2118

WAR DIARY
or
INTELLIGENCE SUMMARY
(Erase heading not required.)

Instructions regarding War Diaries and Intelligence Summaries are contained in F. S. Regs., Part II. and the Staff Manual respectively. Title Pages will be prepared in manuscript.

Place	Date	Hour	Summary of Events and Information	Remarks and references to Appendices
	1/10/18		Headquarters Stationed at 28J I.9.c.7.6	
	"		No.1 Section " " " I.9.c.1.8	
	"		No.2 Section " " " I.10.c.6.8	
	"		S.A.A. " " " I.9.D.7.0	
	13/10/18		S.A.A. " on Detachment under Division Q	
	14/10/18		Headquarters moved to 28J K.9.c.8.9	
	"		No.1 Section " " " K.9.a.9.2	
	"		No.2 Section " " " K.17.c.5.8	
	16/10/18		Major Anthony Delegate by the Field Marshall Commanding in Chief the II Corps Commander awarded No 102466 Bdr Almond C. PP the Military Medal for Gallantry and Devotion to Duty in the Field.	
	"		Headquarters moved to BARAKKEN " L.5.c.3.8 (Sheet 28)	
	17/10/18		No.1 Section " " " L.5.c.3.8 (Sheet 28)	
	"		No.2 Section " " " F.29.c.9.9 "	
	18/10/18		Headquarters moved to HEULE	
	21/10/18		" " STACEGHEM	
	"		No.1 Section " " " G.18.c.5.8 (Sheet 29)	
	"		No.2 " " " " G.17.B.5.0 "	
	23/10/18		No.1 Section " " " H.17.c.3.2 "	
	"		No.2 " " " " H.27.a.5.6 "	
	27/10/18		Headquarters " " " W.21.c.20.6.5 (Sheet 28)	

1875 Wt. W593/826 1,000,000 4/15 J.B.C. & A. A.D.S.S./Forms/C. 2118.

WAR DIARY
or
INTELLIGENCE SUMMARY
(Erase heading not required.)

Army Form C. 2118

Place	Date	Hour	Summary of Events and Information	Remarks and references to Appendices
	27/10/18		No 1 Section moved to W.27.c.9.7 (Sheet 28)	
	"		No 2 " " " W.22.c.5.5 "	
	31/10/18		Headquarters Stationed at W.21.c.30.65 (Sheet 28)	
			No 1 Section " W.27.c.9.7 " "	
			No 2 Section " W.22.c.5.5 " "	

[signature]
Lieut.
for Lieut. Colonel.
Comdg. 29 Divisional Ammunition Column

War Diary

29th Divl Ammn Column

vol

November 1918

WAR DIARY

PLACE	DATE	HOUR	SUMMARY OF EVENTS	REMARKS
In the Field	1/11/18		Headquarters Stationed at W 21 c. 30.65 (Sheet 28)	
			No 1 Section " " W 27 c 9 7 "	
			No 2 Section " " W 27 c 5 5 "	
	3/11/18		No 3 Section on Detachment with 19th Div Q	
	7/11/18		Headquarters, No 1, 2 & 3 Sections moved to Toureoing	
	10/11/18		Headquarters No 1 & 2 Sections " " Zwecotin	
	13/11/18		Headquarters No 1 - 2 " " " St Genois	
	14/11/18		Headquarters No 1 - 2 " " " Lille	
	16/11/18		Headquarters No 1 - 2 " " " Moderq	
	19/11/18		Headquarters No 1 - 2 and 3 Sections moved to Ollignies	
	21/11/18		Headquarters No 1 - 2 " 3 " " Petit Enghien	
	22/11/18		Headquarters No 1 - 2 " 3 " " Braine le Chateau	
	25/11/18		Headquarters No 1 - 2 " 3 " " Mont St Etienne	
	27/11/18		Headquarters No 1 - 2 " 3 " " Jauquies St Lambert	
	29/11/18		Headquarters No 1 - 2 " 3 " " Hambraine	
	30/11/18		Headquarters No 1 - 2 " 3 " " Silenry	
	30/11/18		Headquarters No 1 - 2 " 3 " " Coutich Spermes	
			No 1 - 2 " 3 Sections Stationed at Courtlass Spermes	

CONFIDENTIAL

WAR DIARY

OF

29th Armoured Ammunition Column

From 1/11/18 To 31/12/18

Volume No 32

Army Form C. 2118.

WAR DIARY
or
INTELLIGENCE SUMMARY.
(Erase heading not required.)

Instructions regarding War Diaries and Intelligence Summaries are contained in F.S. Regs., Part II. and the Staff Manual respectively. Title pages will be prepared in manuscript.

Place	Date	Hour	Summary of Events and Information	Remarks and references to Appendices
COMBLAIN FAIRON	11/2/18		Headquarters No 1,2 and SAA Section stations at COMBLAIN FAIRON	
AYWAILLE	4/12/18		" " " " " moved to AYWAILLE	
STAVELOT	5/12/18		" " " " " " " STAVELOT	
"	6/12/18		" " " " " " " "	
MALMEDY	7/12/18		" " " " " " " MALMEDY (Germany)	
KALTERHERBERG	8/12/18		" " " " " " " KALTERHERBERG	
SIMMERATH	9/12/18		" " " " " " " SIMMERATH	
ZULPICH	10/12/18		" " " " " " " ZULPICH	
BARRENRATH	11/12/18		" " " " " " " BARRENRATH	
SELBRUCH	12/12/18		" " " " " " " SELBRUCH	
BERG GLADBACH	13/12/18		" " " " " " " BERG GLADBACH	
BERG GLADBACH	14/12/18		Stations at BERG GLADBACH	

LIEUT. COLONEL.
COMDG. 29 DIVISIONAL AMMUNITION COLUMN

RHINE ARMY
SOUTHERN DIVISION
LATE 29TH DIVISION

DIVISIONAL AMMUNITION COLUMN
JAN - OCT 1919

Box 2064 / 2064

AG U 37

Jan – Oct '19

Confidential

War Diary of 29th Div. Ammn. Col.
from 1st to 31st Jany. 1918.
Volume No. 33

Army Form C. 2118.

WAR DIARY
or
INTELLIGENCE SUMMARY.
(Erase heading not required.)

Instructions regarding War Diaries and Intelligence Summaries are contained in F. S. Regs., Part II. and the Staff Manual respectively. Title pages will be prepared in manuscript.

Place	Date	Hour	Summary of Events and Information	Remarks and references to Appendices
Burg-Gladbach	1/1/19		Headquarters No's 1, 2 and S.A.A. Sections stationed at Burg-Gladbach	
"	31/1/19		" 1, 2 " S.A.A. " " Burg Gladbach	

Weisley Lieut
for LIEUT. COLONEL,
Comdg. 29 - DIVISIONAL AMMUNITION COLUMN.

T2134. Wt. W708-776. 500000. 4/15. Sir J. C. & S.

Confidential.

WAR DIARY

of

29th Divisional Ammunition Column.

February 1919.

VOLUME XXXVII.

Army Form C. 2118.

WAR DIARY
or
INTELLIGENCE SUMMARY.
(Erase heading not required.)

Instructions regarding War Diaries and Intelligence Summaries are contained in F. S. Regs., Part II. and the Staff Manual respectively. Title pages will be prepared in manuscript.

Place	Date	Hour	Summary of Events and Information	Remarks and references to Appendices
Berg. Gladbach	1,2,9		Headquarters, No's 1, 2 & SAA Section stationed at Berg. Gladbach	
"	28/2/19		" 1, 2 & SAA " " Berg. Gladbach.	

W B Oates
for LIEUT. COLONEL
of DIVISIONAL AMMUNITION

T2134. Wt. W708—776. 500000. 4/15. Sir J. C. & S.

Army Form C. 2118.

WAR DIARY
or
INTELLIGENCE SUMMARY.
(Erase heading not required.)

Southern D.A.C.

Place	Date	Hour	Summary of Events and Information	Remarks and references to Appendices
Berg Gladbach	1/5/19		Headquarters Nos 1-2 & S.A.A. Section at Berg Gladbach	
"	17/5/19		No 1 section moved to Paffrath	
"	"		" " " stationed at Paffrath	
"	31/5/19		Headquarters No 2 & S.A.A. Section stationed at Berg Gladbach.	

G.J. Kennard 2/Lieut R.F.A
for. O.C. Southern Divisional Ammunition Column.

Army Form C. 2118.

WAR DIARY
or
INTELLIGENCE SUMMARY.   Southern D.A.C.
(Erase heading not required.)

Instructions regarding War Diaries and Intelligence Summaries are contained in F. S. Regs., Part II. and the Staff Manual respectively. Title pages will be prepared in manuscript.

Place	Date	Hour	Summary of Events and Information	Remarks and references to Appendices
Berg Gladbach	1-6-19		Headquarters No 2 & 3 D.A.C. Section at Berg Gladbach. No 1 Section at Paffrath	
"	30-6-19		" " " " " " " " " " " "	

J. Kennedy, Capt. R.F.A. ADJUTANT
SOUTHERN DIVISIONAL AMMUNITION COLUMN

HEADQUARTERS
SOUTHERN DIVISION
AMMUNITION COLUMN
No.
Date 30/6/19

Army Form C. 2118.

WAR DIARY
or
INTELLIGENCE SUMMARY.
(Erase heading not required.)

Instructions regarding War Diaries and Intelligence Summaries are contained in F. S. Regs., Part II. and the Staff Manual respectively. Title pages will be prepared in manuscript.

Place	Date	Hour	Summary of Events and Information	Remarks and references to Appendices
	1-7-19		No 1 Section at Rafgrath	
	" "		No 2 Section A.A of Headquarters at Berg Gladbach.	
	31-7-19		" " "	
	" "		No 1 Section at Rafgrath	
	16-7-19		Captain T.F. ARCHBOLD posted to Southern D.A.C.	
	31-7-19		2/Lieut E. CORSCADEN Demobilized	

HEADQUARTERS
SOUTHERN DIVISION
AMMUNITION COLUMN
No.
Date 31-7-19

J. Heannt Captain R.F.A.
ADJUTANT
SOUTHERN DIVISIONAL AMMUNITION COLUMN.

Army Form C. 2118.

WAR DIARY
or
INTELLIGENCE SUMMARY.
(Erase heading not required.)

Instructions regarding War Diaries and Intelligence Summaries are contained in F. S. Regs., Part II. and the Staff Manual respectively. Title pages will be prepared in manuscript.

Place	Date	Hour	Summary of Events and Information	Remarks and references to Appendices
BERGISCH GLADBACH	31.8.19		Headquarters, Nos 2 & 3 Sections	
PAFFRATH	"		No 1. SECTION	
BERGISCH GLADBACH	19.8.19		Lieut-Colonel E.W. Spedding C.M.G. R.F.A relinquished command of Southern Division of Army of Occupation	
	1884		Capt. W.C. Heath R.F.A (O.C. No 2 Section) left for demobilisation	

C.W.H. Capt. R.F.A
LIEUT. COLONEL
CMDG. SOUTHERN DIVISIONAL AMMUNITION C[OLUMN]

Army Form C. 2118.

WAR DIARY
or
INTELLIGENCE SUMMARY.
(Erase heading not required.)

Instructions regarding War Diaries and Intelligence Summaries are contained in F. S. Regs., Part II. and the Staff Manual respectively. Title pages will be prepared in manuscript.

Place	Date	Hour	Summary of Events and Information	Remarks and references to Appendices
BERGISCH GLADBACH	30.9.19		Headquarters, Nos 2 & 3 Sections Southern D.A.C.	
PAFFRATH	30.9.19		No 1 Section Southern D.A.C.	
BERGISCH GLADBACH	8.9.19		LIEUT-COLONEL J.R. COLVILLE D.S.O. R.F.A. assumed Command of Southern D.A.C. on posting from England.	
"	12.9.19		LIEUT/CAPT SMITH H. R.F.A. assumed command of SAA Section on posting from 126 Brigade R.F.A.	
"	18.9.19		LIEUT/A/CAPT MULLINS F. R.F.A. relinquished command of SAA Section to proceed for dispersal in U.K.	
"	22.9.19		LIEUT. H.W.H. DYKE. R.F.A. to Southern Divisional Schools as Instructor	
			LEAVE	
	25.9.19		CAPT T.T. ARCHBOLD R.F.A. In charge of Advance Draft (SPECIAL) 25.9.19 to 22.9.19	
	25.9.19		LT J. MAPPIN Ditto (SPECIAL) 19.9.19 to 19.10.19	
	24.9.19		LT E.A. BURNER (ORDINARY) 1.9.19 - 15.9.19	
	19.9.19		LT H. KING 1.9.19 - 15.9.19	
			LT H.M. GIBBS 3.9.19 - 17.9.19	
	3.9.19		2/LT W.F. WILSDON 8.9.19 - 22.9.19	
	22.8.19		LT H. DISLEY 6.9.19 - 20.9.19	
	2.9.19		LT H.A. JOHNSON 11.9.19 - 25.9.19	
	7.9.19		2/LT J.C. STEPHENS 16.9.19 - 30.9.19	
	3.9.19		LT L.F. CLANCY 17.9.19 - 1.10.19	
	15.9.19		LT C.W. STRINGER	
	16.9.19		2/LT J.P. HODGKINSON	

CMDG. SOUTHERN DIVISIONAL AMMUNITION COLUMN.
for LIEUT COLONEL

Army Form C. 2118.

WAR DIARY
or
INTELLIGENCE SUMMARY.
(Erase heading not required.)

Instructions regarding War Diaries and Intelligence Summaries are contained in F. S. Regs., Part II. and the Staff Manual respectively. Title pages will be prepared in manuscript.

Place	Date	Hour	Summary of Events and Information	Remarks and references to Appendices
Reng-Gladbach	21.10.19		Headquarters, No 2, No 3 and S.A.A. Section Southern D.A.C.	
Dalpach.	31.10.19		No. 1. Section. Southern. D.A.C.	
Eng-Gladbach	19.10.19		2nd/Lieut J. C. Plickers proceeded to U.K. for disposal.	
	10.10.19		2nd/Lieut P. J. Miller joined for regimental only	
	11.10.19		Lieut H. G. Pearson " " "	
	22.10.19		Lieut E. A. Byrne proceeded to U.K. for disposal.	
	23.10.19		Lieut K. A. Johnson " " "	
	25.10.19		Lieut L. H. Clancy " " "	
	23.10.19		Lieut C. W. Stringer " " "	
	25.10.19		Lieut R. Greenfield joined for regimental duty from Northern. D.A.	
	25.10.19		Lieut L. G. Russell " " " " Northern Light D.A.	
	23.10.19		Lieut F. P. Gillimore " " " " Southern Divisional "	
	24.10.19		Lieut A. J. King assumed command of Southern Divisional Maker.	
	25.10.19		Section J. C. Lancaster D.A.C. joined Southern D.A.C. and became No 3 Section for transport	
	26.10.19		Capt. J. B. R. Harley Commanding the 3 Section joined Southern D.A.	
	28.10.19		Lieut H. W. Boyd joined Southern D.A.C. and became D.A. for regimental only	
	28.10.19		2nd/Lieut F. G. Willoughby " " "	
	26.10.19		2nd/Lieut W. A. Ryle " " "	
	29.10.19		Lieut J. Mappin proceeded to U.K. for disposal	
	29.10.19		2nd/Lieut J. P. Houghton " " "	
	30.10.19		Capt F. J. Critchfield " " "	
	30.10.19		2nd/Lieut H. W. Hooney joined for regimental duty from Lowbank. D.A.	
	31.10.19		Lieut W. W. Taylor " " "	
	31.10.19		Lieut J. W. Elio " " "	

J. Clemons
LIEUT. COLONEL
CMDG. SOUTHERN DIVISIONAL AMMUNITION COLUMN.

www.ingramcontent.com/pod-product-compliance
Lightning Source LLC
Chambersburg PA
CBHW081553160426
43191CB00011B/1918